Choral Evensong

A User's Guide

— ANDREW GREGORY —

Sacristy
Press

Sacristy Press
PO Box 612, Durham, DH1 9HT

www.sacristy.co.uk

First published in 2025 by Sacristy Press, Durham

Sacristy Limited, registered in England
& Wales, number 7565667

British Library Cataloguing-in-Publication Data
A catalogue record for the book is
available from the British Library

ISBN 978-1-78959-420-1

Contents

Acknowledgments

This introduction to Choral Evensong is based on reflections developed during 20 years of participation in Choral Evensong at University College, Oxford. I am grateful to students, colleagues and guests who have joined me there on a Sunday evening, among them our former and current Directors of Music, Kathryn Burningham and Giles Underwood, and all who are or have been members of our chapel choir and wider congregation. I thank them for their contribution to our corporate life, and for all that I have received through their participation in our worship at Evensong and on other occasions. Some of those people have heard and discussed earlier versions of parts of what I have written here, and I am grateful to them for their comments and questions.

I am pleased also to record my thanks to successive Masters and Fellows of the College for their support for the Chapel and for me as Chaplain, and for giving me time and other help to publish this book. Thanks also to those who read or commented on some or all of it, among them Matthew Cheung-Salisbury, Paul King and Robert Morgan.

St Patrick's Day
17 March 2025

Introduction

The cultural resonance of Choral Evensong extends far beyond the churches, chapels and cathedrals in which it is sung. The well-known scientist and "new atheist" Richard Dawkins admits to "a certain love" for the service. The radio and TV presenter, and former pop-star, the Revd Richard Coles, takes it as a reference point in the title of his novel, *Murder after Evensong*. A journalist and music critic, writing in a broadsheet newspaper not known for its defence of religious views, describes it as "one of England's richest heritages—a living tradition that costs precisely nothing to experience live". Even in an age in which increasing numbers of people in England describe themselves as non-religious, there is something about Choral Evensong that continues to touch those who experience it in a way that many other forms of Christian worship or expressions of Christian belief do not. And that is what this book is about.

For me, Choral Evensong has for more than twenty years played a central part in my professional life and in my personal practice of prayer and worship. The earliest experiences of Choral Evensong that I remember were occasional and sporadic, when from time to time I attended a midweek service in the beautiful but austere setting of Durham Cathedral. I did not know the service well, so my thoughts were more often on what might happen next, and whether I should sit, stand or kneel, than on what the service might offer. Similar anxieties were compounded when first I found myself having to conduct the service as a college chaplain, with responsibility for guiding others through a structure that still felt unfamiliar and intimidating. I remember falling at almost the first hurdle, when the student conducting the choir looked at me to say "over to you", and I looked at him wondering why he was not directing the choir to sing. He was right, and I was wrong, as I came to realize. So after an awkward silence, that cannot have been nearly as long as it felt, the service continued and together we said the Lord's Prayer.

To put it another way, Choral Evensong is not an immediately accessible service. It can take some getting used to. But as I have grown into it, and seen others do the same, I have become increasingly aware of what it has to offer, and how it may embrace those who feel able to relax into it as they grow accustomed to its content and form. How, to quote the historian Diarmaid MacCulloch, "its understated presentation of the sacred may yet be the solace of those who find other, more demonstrative, expressions of Christianity beyond their powers of assent". Therefore, in what follows, I set out to explore how Choral Evensong functions both as Christian worship and as a setting in which people of different faiths or none may find space in which to reflect. No two individuals may experience the service in the same way, and all who attend Evensong may experience it in different ways at different points in their lives, depending on what they bring with them at the time. But I have two broad kinds of reader in mind as I write this book.

The first kind of reader includes people who describe themselves as having no religious belief, yet may attend and enjoy a service such as Evensong. Among them are those who value the opportunity to sing in a choir, or the chance to listen and to reflect while others sing, often in buildings of great beauty that offer a tranquil and appealing space in a busy and frequently stressful world. These readers are people who may value and may practice what MacCulloch calls "evensong spirituality", and who appreciate the way in which the service offers a "performance of patterned liturgical beauty [that] may provide a window on seriousness" in a way to which they may relate. Although they may not think of themselves as religious, they may or may not describe themselves as atheists. Why, they might ask, should anyone expect them to define themselves by reference to not believing in a god or gods the case for whose existence they doubt or reject?

Like most of the students with whom I work, these are readers who would very likely choose the box marked "none" if asked to tick a box indicating to which religion (if any) they belonged or with which they identified. Yet they may value Choral Evensong, even if they are sceptical about religious faith or belief, although not opposed to its cultural expression. They may also be interested in how religion (especially Christianity in one version of its "Anglican" or "Church of England" form) has helped to shape the society in which they live.

If that description sounds a bit like you, I hope that reading this book might contribute to your fuller appreciation of how Evensong functions—that it will help you to appreciate it more fully, without expecting you to change your opinion about any religious or theological claims that either I or the service might make.

The second type of reader is simpler to label, although it too includes a wide range of people: those who describe themselves or who self-identify as Christians, and who engage in Evensong as an act of Christian worship. If that includes you, I hope that reading the book will contribute to your fuller understanding of how the service may enable you to worship God, of how it draws on the Bible to teach us about a Christian understanding of God, and about how Christians believe that they may respond to God's call on their lives. I take seriously the fact that Choral Evensong was designed as an act of worship, in an age when belief in God was taken for granted by most people, and that many of us still find it a means of encountering God today.

All of us share a common humanity that transcends our differences on matters of faith and belief. This book takes seriously shared human needs and experiences as a basis for exploring how the experience of being present at a church service like Choral Evensong can make a difference to those who participate or attend. I hope that its exploration of questions that the service may raise, or claims that it may make, will enhance mutual understanding and respect between people who see and understand the world in different ways. And that this discussion may help to explain why at least some Christians believe in at least some of the things that they do.

1

Work of art and act of worship: Choral Evensong today

Many people who attend Choral Evensong come for the music, whether they sing in the choir, or sit in the wider congregation. For those who appreciate the music, but do not consider themselves religious, the appeal of Choral Evensong may be expressed in terms of an aesthetic experience, or an encounter with something sublime. For others, however, the music contributes to something that may be described as an encounter with God. So the service can be appreciated as a work of art or an act of worship, each enhanced by the often awe-inspiring buildings in which it is sung and heard.

If some come to Evensong almost entirely for the music, others may appreciate the music not as the sole or primary attraction, but as part of a greater aesthetic experience. The quality of the prose, whether said or sung, may be part of this, as may the reflective nature of the service, and the fact that it often takes place in a setting of great architectural beauty, which offers space for contemplation and a welcome respite from the demands of life outside the building. Choral Evensong may offer a sense of sacred space, both in a temporal and in a physical space, in which those who attend may choose to engage as much or as little as they wish—either with the content and form of the service, or with those around them. It can be experienced or understood as a kind of drama or musical theatre in which individuals may participate as part of the cast or the chorus, or as members of the audience.

Both those who understand themselves as religious, and those who identify as atheists, unbelievers, or as "nones", may each encounter Choral Evensong in this aesthetic way. What may set the two groups apart, however, is whether they understand it only in aesthetic terms, or also as an act of Christian worship. For those who take the latter view, the service is not primarily or only an aesthetic experience, but also a means of encountering the glory of the God in whom Christians and other people of faith place their faith and in relation to whom they seek to live their lives and to understand their place in the world.

Whether it is sung in great cathedrals, in school or college chapels, in local parish churches or elsewhere, Choral Evensong continues to attract great devotion. It has been presented as part of the explanation as to why more people are attending weekday services in cathedrals than ever before. But it would be naïve to ignore the fact that this increase in cathedral attendance, and the apparent popularity of Choral Evensong, must be seen in the context of a much larger decline in religious observance in Britain and Ireland, and in other parts of the increasingly post-Christian western world.

Choral Evensong is in origin a Tudor text that developed in an early modern historical context in which belief in God was taken largely for granted. Like the rest of the Book of Common Prayer in which it is found, it was intended to bind together a nation state through a religious faith that all its subjects shared with the monarch who ruled over them. The modern nation states in which Evensong is said or sung today no longer function in that way, so the service cannot bind together the nation in the way that it was once expected to do. Its context has changed, but the ongoing use of the service shows that it continues to have relevance and resonance today, and there is evidence to suggest that interest in it may be growing.

In 2012, there were celebrations to mark the 350th anniversary of the publication of the 1662 version of the Book of Common Prayer, of which Choral Evensong is a part. Such celebrations could easily be interpreted as a way of marking the end of an era, even if that was not what their organizers may have intended. But developments since 2012 indicate the opposite: that Evensong is part of a living heritage, rather than one that may be consigned to the past. In 2016, for example, the BBC marked the 90th anniversary of its weekly broadcast of Choral Evensong. Initially broadcast on the Home Service, which later became Radio 4, it now airs on Radio 3: first, live, on a Wednesday afternoon, and then repeated on Sunday afternoon. It has its own page on the BBC website, is listened to regularly by 250,000 people, and is the BBC's longest running outside broadcast. And the BBC is far from Choral Evensong's only digital home. It has its own site at www.choralevensong.org, which was launched in 2015, and allows users in Britain and Ireland to find a service near them. Having emerged in the English Reformation, and having successfully negotiated the transition from print through analogue to digital media, Choral Evensong continues to be valued and cherished by many people, and for a wide variety of reasons.

2

Performance or participation: The importance of context

Jonathan Arnold, who is both a professional singer and an Anglican priest, has wide experience both in performing music and in leading worship in which music plays an important role. He tells a story which captures some of the differences between music as performance, in the setting of a concert, and music as worship, in the setting of Choral Evensong.

Arnold was at York Minster, having driven there from his home in Oxfordshire, in order to perform a concert of sacred Renaissance music, as a member of the choir, The Sixteen. In the space between a brief rehearsal, and The Sixteen's performance that evening, he took the opportunity to attend Choral Evensong in the Minster. It was an opportunity for him to hear some music, and to participate in the service, but not actually to sing most of the music himself.

He recounts his experience as follows, describing the relatively small-scale setting of the Minster's choir stalls, and the nearness of congregation and choir during the service. The relative intimacy of the service, he notes, would be quite different from his performance later when he would face 1,700 people, most seated at some distance from the stage on which he and the other performers would sing: a platform erected for the purpose of performance, rather than that of worship.

> Far from being tiny figures, as the men and boys of the choir and clergy processed in their flowing robes, I could scrutinize each of their faces, see their folders of music and hear their voices distinctly as they began the Preces and Responses. This was not a concert. Instead, those present were worshipping together, with all that the concept implied: standing, sitting, turning east for the Creed, kneeling to pray—a sort of contract between priest, reader, musician, listener, worshipper and God. The music enhanced the worship, giving beauty and character to the heartfelt words of the Psalms, to the joyful thanksgiving in Mary's song of praise and liberation, the Magnificat, and to the prayers of the Collects. The music of worship was interspersed with words and silence, in which our own thoughts and petitions crept in and became part of the tapestry of the liturgy. The experience was an oasis in my day; not because it was an escapist hour away from the noise of

the street and motorway, but as a participation in something new and other. It was a pointer towards the divine, and a collective expression from all who were there that day of thanks for the gift of life. As the choir and clergy left, I felt glad that I had joined with those fellow worshippers in York. People I did not know and would probably never see again, but with whom I now had a bond forged by the shared experience of that liturgical rite and in what had brought us there.

There are two points in Arnold's account on which I'd like to reflect. The first, which is the reason why he tells the story, is the difference between sacred music when sung in the context of a religious service, and in the context of a performance before an audience who have paid to be there. When he goes on to describe the performance, he notes that the contract was now between performer and audience, that no prayer was required or encouraged, and that while some simply appreciated the music, on a par with other equally fine pieces, others might have had a particular interest in the historical context in which it arose. Yet although Arnold here focuses on what is different when music is sung in worship or as a concert performance, certain similarities may also be noted. No musician or choir member, whether a person of faith or not, wants to perform or to sing any less well than they can. And no one who worships God wants to give any less than their best, whatever that might mean in the circumstances or context in which they find themselves. So when Choral Evensong or any other church service offers people an opportunity to come and sing together they may find a common purpose regardless of whether they profess a common faith. This is why the Church has long been a patron of music and other arts, and why musicians and other artists have long found a valued place in the Church regardless of what they might, or might not, believe.

The second is the way in which Arnold describes himself as having participated in Choral Evensong, even when he was not a member of the choir who sang most of the service. Sometimes, it is said, Choral Evensong is no more than a spectator sport, which requires neither exertion nor involvement on the part of those who come—a musical performance that might bring together the members of the choir, but that excludes those who do not sing the service with them. Yet Arnold's description of his experience points to another perspective. We see this in his claim that he had joined with others in "a collective expression ... of thanks for the gift of life", and his sense that though he joined with strangers for only a short time, yet he had formed with them "a bond forged by the shared experience of that liturgical rite and in what had brought us there". Through their music, the choir had enabled him to participate in an act of worship; the fact that he was not singing with them did not mean that he was excluded from what was going on.

Michael Sadgrove, a former Dean of Durham, sometimes described as Britain's favourite cathedral, makes a similar point. People are wrong, he suggests, to say that Choral Evensong is liturgy, or a form of worship, in which you don't join in. "You do join in", he writes. "But in a contemplative way, by listening, paying attention, allowing yourself to be transported into another place by what you are hearing and experiencing."

As a former boy chorister, and someone who lived or worked in a cathedral for more than thirty years, Sadgrove writes as someone for whom Choral Evensong has helped to shape and structure the shape of his day and the patterns of his prayer for much of his life. Now retired, he still travels to Choral Evensong each week, and still tunes in to BBC Radio 3 on a Wednesday for its live broadcast of Evensong.

Yet not everyone who attends Choral Evensong will experience or understand it in that way, nor would they consider it to be a form of prayer, no matter how much they might value it for other reasons. Instead they may see it as a moment of reflection or rest in the midst of a demanding week, and a time to step aside from the demands that they themselves or other people might place upon them. Rather than a context in which they might forge some sort of bond with others around them, part of its attraction may be that they do not need to sing or speak any of the words found in the service, and so may maintain a certain distance from what those words express. And that they can choose whether to stand or sit when others do, or to remain in the posture that they prefer, and to enter and leave the building with or without engaging or interacting with others who may also be present.

Readers of this book who wish to remain behind a pillar, metaphorical or otherwise, are welcome to do so. If that is you, and your interest in Evensong is aesthetic, I hope that reflection on the structure and content of the service will enhance your appreciation of the historical and religious traditions that have shaped it, even if your experience does not include a sense of shared purpose with those who understand the service as a form of worship.

For other readers, however, those who come to Choral Evensong in the hope of worshipping God, of being drawn into what they might call an encounter with the divine, I hope that the book will be of interest and of use in a different way. That it will not only help to explain the structure and content of the service, and how it came to be as it is usually found today, but also that it will help to show how it may be a useful devotional tool. A way of helping those who attend and experience it to look beyond themselves, to encounter God in worship, and to understand the story of their own lives in relation to the Christian story of God, the world, and all people, that Choral Evensong sets out to tell.

As a former version of the website of Coventry Cathedral used to explain, in an online introduction to Choral Evensong, church services use music of different kinds. Some of it is simple, and allows everyone to sing it. However, on other occasions, like Choral Evensong, the music requires a high level of musical ability and preparation, and gifted musicians lead the worship on behalf of everyone present:

> The idea is that the highly-trained skills of the choir and organist blend with the splendour of this extraordinary building in a service which sets the congregation free to meditate on the words and music and so be lifted into a fuller sense of the reality and power of God. It can take a bit of getting used to, but many people have found that this particular combination of words, music and space really helps them to discover God and open their lives to him.

3

Structure and language: Sounding and hearing the Service

One of the attractions of Choral Evensong is its simple structure and short length. You can say it in 20 minutes, or sing it in 35, so the short core of the service allows lots of music to be added, without distorting its form. "Its script, as it were," writes one historian of church music, "is light enough in weight to permit plenty of musical embellishment without a sense of disproportion". To put it rather crudely, you can pack a lot of music in without making the service too long or unwieldy. Or, in the college context where I work, without making anyone late for dinner after the service. Even with three hymns and a sermon you can be out in about an hour.

Closely tied to this is the balance between familiarity and change. The structure or script is quite simple, so we can get to know it and inhabit it in a way that becomes natural and relaxed. A way that means that we don't need always to be thinking about what happens next. But the music to which familiar words are set is always changing, as are the words of the readings and the words and music of the psalm and the hymns. Within the familiar there is always scope for something that is fresh and new yet stands within a tradition that goes back not just to the origins of Evensong in the English Reformation, or even to the medieval monastic liturgies on which it draws, but back to the more ancient words of Scripture of which it is almost entirely composed. The script allows us, through changing words and music, to focus and to reflect on different themes at different points in the year. And to reflect or express different needs and emotions and hope and fear in response to different life events and to situations as they arise. A structured service, that includes set forms of words (a liturgy) verbalizes thoughts and feelings and gives us statements and claims to which we may give or withhold our assent. In times of pressure or crisis it enables us to articulate what we might not otherwise be able to express.

Evensong, along with Mattins (also known as Morning Prayer), stands in a long tradition of services intended to encourage a regular fixed pattern of daily prayer. In his preface to the 1549 edition of the Book of Common Prayer, Cranmer referred to the pattern of common prayer in Church as "divine service", but the practice of a fixed pattern of daily prayer has been referred to in a number of ways. These include the daily office, the divine office, the canonical hours, and the liturgy of the hours (and are to be distinguished from the form of worship known variously as Holy Communion, the Eucharist, the Lord's Supper or the Mass). Evensong and Mattins each include material from the older forms of daily prayer, said or sung at different points in the day, that were in use in pre-Reformation England and throughout the western Church, both in religious communities and in private homes.

The form of services on which Cranmer drew for Mattins and Evensong was primarily that of the "Sarum use", a form of worship associated with the English Diocese of Salisbury. In the case of Evensong, some material came from the early evening service of Vespers, and some from the service of Compline, designed to be used before sleep. Both Evensong and Mattins remained largely unchanged in later editions of the Book of Common Prayer, and their core structure and contents remain in use today, although with many variations in detail, especially at the beginning and end of each service.

Both Mattins and Evensong follow the same structure, which serves the purpose for which they were written. Each begins and ends with prayers and includes a creed, but at their core is a series of texts designed to facilitate the reading of the Bible, and to evoke an appropriate response. This central part of the service includes one or more psalms and two readings or "lessons" from the Bible, each followed by a "canticle", a hymn of praise that is also drawn directly from Scripture. We shall look in greater depth at these parts of the service in Chapter

6, about the psalms, and in Chapter 5, about the two lessons and the two canticles or biblical hymns of praise that follow them.

Before and after this core of structured reading from the Bible are two other sequences of material. The content and form of the first sequence is the part of the service in which most variation is found today. On a Sunday, Evensong may begin with a hymn, and usually continues with an introductory address in which the minister exhorts those present to confess their sins, confident that God will forgive. If the service follows the 1662 Book of Common Prayer, the introductory address focusses entirely on the need for confession and forgiveness. If instead the service begins with a widely used alternative introduction, drawn from the 1928 Book of Common Prayer, the person leading Evensong still exhorts those present to make confession of their sins, but also calls their attention to other aspects of the service. In both cases, the service continues with words of confession and an absolution or assurance of God's forgiveness (using either the 1662 form, or the form introduced as an alternative in 1928).

The service then continues with the Lord's Prayer, and with a set of short devotional sentences, often known as versicles and responses, which Cranmer drew from earlier forms of daily prayer. When sung, these versicles and responses take the form of a dialogue between the minister or a cantor, to whom the choir responds, on behalf of all those present. When said, the dialogue is between the person leading the service and everyone else. The words of these opening prayers are based on the psalms and they function as an invitation to prayer and a request for God to empower those who worship him:

> *versicle*: O Lord open thou our lips,
> *response*: And our mouth shall shew
>   forth thy praise (cf. Psalm 51:15).
> *versicle*: O God, make speed to save us,
> *response*: O Lord, make haste to
>   help us (cf. Psalm 70:1).

They are then followed by a doxology, or expression of praise, that reflects the distinctively Christian trinitarian understanding of God, and that is repeated after the psalm and the canticles:

> Glory to the Father, and to the Son,
> And to the Holy Ghost;
> As it was in the beginning, is now, and ever shall be:
> World without end. Amen.

This particular formula is sometimes known as the "Lesser Doxology", to distinguish it from the longer text known as the "Great Doxology" or "Greater Doxology". This longer doxology, or structured liturgical formula expressing praise to God, begins "Glory to God in the highest (*Gloria in excelsis*)", which are the words sung by the angels after one of their number announced to the shepherds the birth of Jesus (Luke 2:14). The Book of Common Prayer includes the longer doxology towards the end of its communion service, but it is not used at Evensong.

Then follows the central core of the service in which those present are invited to hear and respond to the Bible, followed by the last part of the service that includes the Creed and further prayers. The positioning of the Creed (on which see further below, Chapter 6) emphasizes that Christian doctrine is based on the Bible, and prepares the way for those present to continue in prayer (on which see further below, Chapters 8 and 9), confident in their faith in the God whom they address. As earlier commentators have put it, "It follows upon the reading of Holy Scripture, the foundation of faith, and precedes prayer, which both needs and sustains faith."

In the final part of the service there is usually an anthem, sung by the choir, and there may also be a hymn. On a Sunday this part of the service will often include a sermon, in which the preacher directly addresses those present, seeking to make connections between Christian faith and daily life, often with reference to one or more of the psalms or Bible readings from earlier in the service. The service ends with the minister pronouncing a blessing and may be followed by an organ voluntary which provides space for further reflection, or an opportunity for those present to depart.

The regular pattern of the service, which is repeated each time it is used, and which mirrors the structure of Mattins, together with the repeated use of certain forms of words (e.g. the Lord's Prayer, the Magnificat, the Nunc Dimittis, versicles and responses and two of the collects) allows participants to grow familiar with and to relax into the service. This means that it can carry them along and enable them to look beyond the service—either to the God whom they worship, or as a way of being in the moment and seeking calm and serenity amidst the demands of daily life. The frequent and repeated use of prayers whose rhythms helps to make them memorable enables those who hear or say them to internalize them, to learn them by heart, and in turn be shaped and centred by them. Texts that vary from day to day or from week to week (e.g. psalms, lessons, the anthem, the first collect and other prayers) help to convey the passing of time through the seasons of the years, and provide variety and new challenges and insights within the unchanging structure of the service.

4

For the continual reading of Scripture: Hearing the Bible in church

Although it was written to encourage a regular fixed pattern of daily prayer, Evensong also has a very specific purpose closely connected with its origins in the English Reformation. Its particular purpose is clearly stated in the preface to the 1549 Book of Common Prayer (which focuses mainly on the two services or "offices" of Morning and Evening Prayer) and is repeated in the more wide-ranging preface found in the edition of 1662. Evensong, like Mattins, is intended to facilitate the orderly and continuous recitation of the Psalms, and the systematic, orderly and structured reading of the Bible.

To show how this should happen, the Prayer Book of 1662 contains two tables, each with an explanatory preface. In the first are instructions as to how the psalms are appointed to be read over the course of each month, which result in two or three psalms being recited at Mattins and at Evensong each day, almost always in the order in which they are found in the Psalter. In the second are instructions as to how most of the Old Testament is to be read once over the course of a year, split up into sections suitable for use as the first lesson (the Prayer Book's term for a reading from the Bible) at Mattins and at Evensong. Also included here are instructions as to how most of the New Testament is to be read three times (with the exception of the Revelation to John, which is read only very selectively, and passages from the Gospels and Epistles which are also read on Sundays at Holy Communion). The order in which the Bible is read midweek at Evensong follows that of the books of the Bible, divided across the calendar year. This may be compared with the selection and of pattern of Bible readings on Sundays that reflects the order and seasons of the Church's year (Advent, Christmas, Lent, Easter, etc.).

Both Mattins and Evensong follow the same structure, as we have noted already. Each begins and ends with prayers and includes a creed, but at their core is a series of elements designed to facilitate the reading of the Bible, and to evoke an appropriate response. This sequence, which gives these services their distinctive Anglican shape, may be set out as follows:

- Psalms
- First Lesson (from the Old Testament)
- Magnificat (a canticle, or song of praise, from Luke 1:46–55)
- Second Lesson (from the New Testament)

- Nunc Dimittis (a canticle, or song of praise, from Luke 2:29–32).

A clear progression may be seen. The use of the psalms (or one psalm, in many services today) helps to root this one particular form of Christian worship in the long history of Jewish and Christian worship. The psalms offer words through which those who use them may articulate and express the whole range of human emotion and experience, all of which they may bring to God. Their regular recital evokes and enacts the belief that part of what it means to be human is to live a life in which we acknowledge our status as creatures, which means living our lives in recognition of our ultimate dependence on God. The use of the psalms at this point in the service provides a context in which may be heard the words of the Bible and its story of the relationship between God and his people and the whole world that God has created. We will explore this further in Chapter 5.

Not surprisingly, the first lesson comes from the Old Testament, the Christian term for the books of the Hebrew Bible, and the first part of the Christian Bible. The first of the 39 books brought together in this collection is Genesis, which sets the scene for all that follows. It begins with an account of creation, better understood not as a rival account or challenge to modern scientific claims about the origin of the universe and the evolution of life on earth, but as a way of making sense of our human experience of life on earth, and why things are as we find them to be. It is a mythical account, so like other myths it is a story that is intended to help to explain the world and why human life is as it is, and that should not be read as a historical narrative or scientific textbook. Not until Genesis Chapter 12 do we move into the realm of what we might think of as human prehistory, when we read of God's call of Abraham and through him a chosen people whose story the rest of the Old Testament recounts. Its different books include forms of historical narrative, short stories about heroes and heroines of the Hebrew people, collections of prophetic oracles, texts that seek to make sense of the world and of human existence, and different explanations as to how best the Hebrew people should follow God's commands in response to his gracious calling of them to be his people.

Next follows the Magnificat, a canticle or song of praise found in the opening chapters of the Gospel according to Luke, where it is placed on the lips of Mary, the mother of Jesus (Luke 1:46–55). Its Latin title means "magnify" in the sense of "make great", "exalt", "extol" or "praise", which comes from its opening line. Mary praises God in response to the news that she is to bear a son, using word and phrases that echo songs of praise found in the Old Testament, for example in the psalms (e.g. 34:3–4; 35:9; 13:5–6; 113) and in Hannah's song of praise for the gift of Samuel her son (1 Samuel 2:1–10). Luke's Greek text of the Magnificat is so similar to the Greek form in which he read the Old Testament that it could almost belong there, along with the rest of the opening two chapters of his Gospel, and that in a way is the point. Mary praises God for all that he has done in the past, and recognizes that through her son God will act again in the future. Thus, in its setting in Choral Evensong, the Magnificat serves to bring the Old and New Testaments together, affirming the Christian claim that the creator God if Israel is the same God who is at work through Jesus Christ. Mary's hymn of praise, itself drawn from the New Testament, sets the scene for the Second Lesson, just as the psalms set the scene for the First.

The Second Lesson consists of texts drawn from the 27 early Christian writings that are included in the New Testament, the second part of the Christian Bible. These include four accounts of the life of Jesus (the Gospels), a narrative about the spread of the early Church (the Acts of the Apostles), a record of a vision in which the risen Jesus appears to one of his followers (the Revelation to John), and a number of letters written by or attributed to Paul and other early followers of Jesus. The letters of Paul are the earliest Christian writings to survive. They show how he set out to explain what he understood to be the universal significance of Jesus and his death and resurrection, even before the Gospel writers (often referred to as evangelists) produced their accounts of Jesus, which tell us much more about his life and ministry than do the letters of Paul or other authors.

None of these texts are neutral accounts, giving merely factual accounts of what Jesus's first followers learned from him, nor are they intended to be. This does not mean that they are not rich historical sources for the development of the early Jesus movement, and historians continue to sift through them today, drawing on them as valuable sources in their attempts to understand and reconstruct the past. But those who wrote them wrote to persuade their readers (or more likely hearers, since these were texts written to be read aloud to audiences that included many who could not read for themselves) of the life-transforming significance of Jesus as the one through whom the God of Israel had acted in a new and decisive way.

Thus those early authors might have approved of Cranmer's decision to refer to extracts from their writings not simply or neutrally as "readings" but rather as "lessons", texts designed to give practical and life-changing instruction to those who hear them and take them to heart. It is possible of course, even in a setting like Choral Evensong, to see these writings only as witnesses to the faith and belief of an earlier age. But by presenting them in a liturgical context, the Church claims that the books of the New Testament, and the Bible as a whole, are also more than that, and that the appropriate response to their claims is one of worship and acknowledgement of how God is at work even today through Jesus, and the Nunc Dimittis gives an example of what such a response might involve.

Like the Magnificat, the Nunc Dimittis also comes from the opening chapters of Luke (Luke 2:29–32). In this case, the person who says these words is Simeon, an elderly man whom Luke introduces as a righteous, devout and Spirit-inspired figure who was looking for the consolation of Israel, and to whom it had been revealed that he would see the Lord's anointed one, the Messiah, before he died. Simeon encounters the infant Jesus when his parents being him to the Temple in Jerusalem, and Simeon stands in the Temple, holding the infant Jesus in his arms, as he utters these words. He asks God that he will now send him away (*"nunc dimittis"*) in peace, for he has seen enough to know that God is at work in Jesus, who will bring salvation not only for Israel but for all the people of the world. Simeon's words, like Mary's, link the New Testament and its stories of God at work in and through Jesus to the Old Testament and its stories of God at work in and through the people of Israel, but where Mary looked back Simeon now looks forward.

In its setting in Choral Evensong, the Nunc Dimittis underlines that the central message of the New Testament, read as the Second Lesson, is of the salvation that God offers through Jesus Christ. And it invites those who sing or hear its words to entrust themselves to God, just as Simeon did, but now with the knowledge of how Jesus has already fulfilled the promise of God in which Simeon had placed his hope. These words offer encouragement and hope for the present and for the future and provide the context in which the service summarizes the main claims of the Christian faith in the words of the Apostles' Creed.

5

Said or sung: Expressing emotions through the Psalms

As the title page of the Book of Common Prayer makes clear, Cranmer and the compilers envisaged that psalms could be said or sung. Both approaches appear to go back to the earliest use of these ancient Hebrew texts, as reflected in different parts of the Bible, and the continuing use of the psalms roots Choral Evensong in a long tradition of Jewish and Christian worship.

In some churches, chapels and cathedrals, only one or two psalms, or sometimes only a portion of a psalm, are sung at most Evensongs. In these places, the choice of the psalm follows a modern lectionary, which distinguishes between psalms that seem more suited for use in the evening or the morning, and also takes account of the time of year. Some psalms feature on a regular basis, while others are not used at all, for reasons that we will consider below.

In other places where the psalms are sung, they continue to be sung in the quantity that Cranmer intended, with the whole Psalter (more or less) sung in the course of each month, in consecutive order without regard for the time of day or the time of year, with only a few exceptions.

The difference between the two approaches is only one of a number of ways in which the recitation or singing of the psalms has developed since they were given the prominent place that they continue to have in Evensong today. The psalms were likely heard in England from the time when Christianity first arrived, and the practice of their being sung goes back at least to the time of Henry II, in the twelfth century. But it was with the arrival of French and Dutch Protestant refugees in the sixteenth century, who brought with them their tradition of chanting psalms, that something like the use of psalms, as found today at Evensong, took off.

The way in which the psalms are sung has changed in different ways since then, but three factors in particular have shaped its development from the sixteenth century until today. One, familiar already to those refugees who fled to London, was the insistence of the Reformers that the psalms be used in such a way that every word could be heard, and that everyone could understand what was being sung.

The second factor is the language in which the psalms are said or sung. Modern service books and bibles include their own translations of the psalms, but the version still used in 1662 Choral Evensong today is almost invariably that of the English translator Miles

Coverdale, on whose version of the psalms Cranmer drew in the first prayer book of 1549. It remained there in later editions, notwithstanding even the publication of the Authorized Version of the Bible (also known as the King James Bible) in 1604, so it is in Coverdale's words that many people know the psalms today. Its rhythmical structure for each psalm, which reflects the medieval tradition of singing Latin psalms to plainchant, was undoubtedly one element in its success. Another, at least initially, may have been the appeal of its familiarity to those who already knew it from the Great Bible of 1539, together with its echoes of the Latin Bible which was one of the major sources on which Coverdale drew. Both elements, together with the simple fact that the Coverdale version was available and ready for use, probably influenced Cranmer's decision to include it in the Prayer Book of 1549, and its rhythm and memorable turns of phrase have helped it to retain its place at Evensong ever since.

The third factor was the publication in 1930 of Sidney Nicholson's *Parish Psalter with Chants*, which is still in use today. It captured in print a new method of chanting psalms with the same rhythm as if they were said, which came to be known as "speech-rhythm chant" or "Anglican chant". Choirs could be heard singing the psalms in this new way on broadcasts of Choral Evensong on the Home Service, and the Royal School of Church Music released a number of gramophone records. One of these records included a recording of Nicholson himself, who explained the new approach. He suggested that parish churches sing along to these recordings in order to help them adapt to this new approach of singing without strict time, and that they chant each syllable with the same emphasis it would receive when spoken. To chant in this way is more difficult than it sounds which is why, at Evensong today, most congregations listen while a carefully rehearsed and trained choir sings the psalms and also some other parts of the service.

In a guide to the Book of Common Prayer, first published in 1912, the authors observe that "one of the beauties of the liturgy is its variety", and that "after the active devotion of Psalmody" (by which they mean congregational singing) "there comes a refreshing repose in listening to the Lessons". Today's choirs may still enjoy the rest that the Lessons offer between their singing the psalms and the canticles, but for those not in the choir the whole block of material that stretches from the psalms to the Nunc Dimittis provides an opportunity for listening or reflection as others sing and read, and an opportunity for as much or as little engagement with the words that are spoken or sung as each person present may choose.

Cranmer's vision was for the whole of the Psalter to be used, and used regularly, so it is worth reflecting on what such an all-embracing or non-discriminating approach to the Psalter might entail, and to compare it with the more selective way in which only parts of the Psalter are often used today.

Modern Psalters put certain texts in square brackets, because what they say is considered problematic or unsuitable for private devotion or for use in public worship, for reasons that are easy to see. Among these difficult and disturbing texts are various imprecatory or curse psalms, in which the psalmist (speaking either as an individual, or on behalf of a community) denounces those whom he sees as his enemies, or implores God to punish them. They call for violence, and depict the psalmist's wish for vengeance against others in graphic terms—not only that his enemies die young (Psalm 109:8), but that their wives be left as widows and their orphaned children be reduced to begging (Psalm 109:9–10), that children have their teeth knocked out (Psalm 58:6) and that babies have their heads smashed against rocks (Psalm 137:9). These are "texts of terror" on any reckoning, but particularly disturbing in worship directed towards a God whose son told his followers to turn the other cheek, and to love their enemies as themselves (Matthew 5:38–48).

So what if anything might we do with texts like this, whether in a context of public worship like Choral Evensong, or in individual reading of the Bible? The first way to try to wrestle with such texts may be to ask why they were written, and why earlier generations may have thought them worth preserving. These are texts that speak with a level of raw emotion that many of us may find disturbing and that exhibit a sense of self-righteousness coupled with hatred for those whom the psalmist considers other that most of us who read, sing or hear the psalms can barely begin to comprehend.

But the fact that the perspective of the psalmist may be so different from our own, and presumably shaped by an experience far removed from our own, is precisely why it may be so important to seek to hear and understand these psalms rather than rushing to condemn or to exclude them. Few of us have been in exile in Babylon, victims of ethnic cleaning, or refugees forced to flee from their homes in the face of hostile forces. Few of us have watched others queue outside the gas chambers, never to return, or have felt the heat of the incinerators as we disposed of their remains. Few of us have cradled a loved one in our arms as he or she died as the victim of a terrorist attack or of a street robbery that went wrong.

If we do not want to join the psalmist in his cries for vengeance, and do not share his burning desire for revenge, it may not be out of any positive virtue, Christian or otherwise. It may be simply that we have not had the particular misfortune to suffer in the way or to the degree that countless others have. If, however, we hear these texts at Choral Evensong, even sung by angelic-sounding choristers, we are reminded of the needs and experiences of others whose lives and circumstances are very different from our own, and we may be prompted to pray for those who suffer today, and perhaps to ask what we might do to alleviate the suffering that they endure.

Often also neglected are psalms that focus not on praise but on lament. It is easy to assume that words used in worship must always be upbeat and positive, a sort of Christian equivalent to the secular insistence on a happy outward appearance that has been lampooned as "smile or die". Yet most people, at some point in their lives, experience darkness and pain of many different kinds—physical, mental and spiritual—and to overlook psalms of individual or community lament may deprive them of forms of prayer that they may use when they have no words of their own to express to God what they feel. When we hear these psalms sung, we may be reminded how others may feel, or given words to express some of what we may feel ourselves. Like the imprecatory psalms, psalms of lament remind us that no experience or emotion is too terrible to be brought to God in prayer, and that public worship needs to account for the whole range of human emotion and experience if it is to be of any use in the world in which we live.

Of course—I hope—there are times when each of us may wish to acknowledge and celebrate the good things in our lives and in the world about us. Many of the psalms give us words in which we can express and articulate our sense of gratitude, and address our thanks and praise to God if we are people of faith. Psalms of praise and thanksgiving are those that we use most often in public worship, and they too can take us beyond ourselves not only in their address to God but also if we note how many are communal rather than individual.

They remind us of the network of communities and relationships in which we live our lives—that "No man is an island, entire of itself" as John Donne, former Dean of St Pauls in London, so famously put this point.

6

Rehearse the articles of thy belief:
What we do when we say the Creed

Part of the attraction of Choral Evensong is the way in which the choir plays such an active role. For much of the service, this provides a reflective space in which others may opt in or opt out as much as they wish, making the words that they hear their own, or allowing them to drift over them as they experience what is sung. In a service full of music, the Creed stands out very sharply. Not only is it part of the service that is almost always said, but it offers a form of words that all present are invited to say. Furthermore, it is a form of words that seems to ask for a level of personal and individual commitment that goes beyond anything else in the service, for at Evensong it begins with the short but insistent word "I".

It is hardly surprising therefore that many who come to Choral Evensong find the Creed one of the most challenging or difficult parts of the service. With no music in which to envelop them, the force of its words seems more insistent because they are said and not sung.

As a consequence, we may feel compelled to reflect on these words and their literal meaning in a way that we do not focus on words elsewhere in the service, where it is easier to understand them as conveying an impression or a mood rather than staking a claim to belief. Yet the form of the Creed seems to do precisely that: to set out a list of propositions or statements to which we are invited to subscribe in the opening words "I believe". What are we doing when or if we join in saying the Creed? And is it entirely or even primarily about intellectual assent?

The Creed used at Choral Evensong is known as the Apostles' Creed. Like other parts of the service, it is an earlier text that Cranmer took from elsewhere and used to construct his new format for daily prayer. It was used in the western medieval services of Prime and Compline, and in the Sarum Use it was said inaudibly by the priest alone, until he raised his voice at the closing words "and life everlasting", so signalling to the choir that they were to join with him in that final clause. It was first known in its present form in the eighth century, but its roots are much older as it likely originates in early baptismal creeds, found in second-century texts. Those early predecessors of the Apostles' Creed draw on creed-like statements found in some books of the New Testament, so it is a statement of faith that goes back to the earliest written Christian texts. Its origin as a baptismal confession of faith explains its use of the first person singular "I believe", for each person to be baptized was required to state his or her own faith, and his or her wish to follow Christ.

There can be no way of avoiding the element of personal commitment encapsulated by the opening two words of the Creed, and many who speak those words will wish to declare, without embarrassment or hesitation, that they as individuals believe what the Creed sets out. Yet the claims that it sets out can never be restricted to merely individual belief, for both the history of the Creed and its use in corporate worship point to its status as a public statement of the central claims of the Christian faith. These claims are something that the whole Church—not just the Church of England—has come to recognize through time and that it continues to declare today. Individuals may engage with them in different ways, in the light of their own place and experience in the world, and in the light of their own belief and understanding, but are not free to change what the Creed set forth. The Apostles' Creed sets out in summary form central Christian beliefs, and an understanding of the world to which those beliefs give rise, which does not depend on any one person assenting to all its parts.

Even if as an individual I may have doubts or questions about a particular part or parts of the Creed—and that part or those parts may change over time—the invitation to recite it in the context of public worship, along with other people, serves also as a reminder that it is more than a matter of individual belief. Philosophers sometimes speak of language as having a performative function, by which they mean that the very act of saying words in a particular context can bring about or enact some form of change in the person who speaks, or in the situation that they address. So to join with others in saying these words may be to say that we belong, or even that we wish to belong, with the people whose faith the Creed sets out. That we want to be in some form of relationship with them: as full members of the Christian Church, as critical friends, or as curious or interested observers and fellow travellers along the way. This is why the manner in which the Creed is introduced may be so important. Those who lead Choral Evensong lead it in different ways, but I myself introduce the Creed by inviting those present to "declare the faith of the Church". Not everyone who is present may wish to say that they believe in what the Creed sets out. But all can affirm without hesitation or compromise that the Creed encapsulates the faith of the Church. Those who wish to can declare the faith of the Church, whether or not they consider that faith to be their own.

It may also be useful to reflect on what is meant by the English word "believe", before turning briefly to the content of the beliefs that the Apostles' Creed sets out. The noun "creed" comes from the Latin verb *credo*, which is usually translated "I believe", and is the opening word of the Creed in its Latin form. Part of its meaning is propositional "belief", in the sense of giving intellectual assent that a certain statement or claim is true. For example, we may believe in the importance of democracy, in the principle of equality before the Law, in gravity, or in the Second Law of Thermodynamics. These are things to which we may give our intellectual assent, and which may have consequences for how we understand the world, and how we live our lives in it.

But the meaning of "belief" is wider than intellectual assent. This may be seen in other ways in which we may use the English verb "believe" and becomes clearer still when we note that *credo* (like the corresponding term in the Greek New Testament) means more than belief. It may be translated not only as "I believe that" or "I believe in", but also as "I trust in", "I trust that" or "I put my confidence in". For to believe or trust in someone is to place our confidence in them and may imply a relationship with them. It is not reducible to a matter of intellectual confidence or assent and may suggest a form of commitment that may be transformative for the person who believes and trusts and has faith in the other. And transformative too for the person who is affirmed, when someone else places their trust, or faith, or belief, in them. All of us know how good it can feel when someone else puts their trust in us. And all of us know how liberating or how frightening it can be when we put our trust in someone else, for it can make us both secure and yet vulnerable all at once.

So understood, saying "I believe" may be as much, if not more, a statement of trust or of faith than a matter of intellectual assent. And Christian faith may be like that:

less a matter of knowing exactly what we believe, than having confidence in the one in whom we might place our trust as we seek to find our way in the world and how best to live our lives. For even if we have difficulty with particular Christian beliefs, it may be possible to place our trust in God, to step out in faith, and to find that that world makes sense if we do.

For some who follow Jesus, their faith begins as a matter of intellectual conviction. It is a conclusion reached by the mind, and is based on careful consideration of adequate evidence, whether historical, philosophical, or theological in nature. For others, it begins with the confidence of the heart based on an experience that has been tried and not found wanting. It involves stepping out in faith, even if questions remain, and finding that faith makes sense of the world, and gives meaning and purpose to our lives.

The author C. S. Lewis put it like this, in words now inscribed on his memorial stone at Poets' Corner in London's Westminster Abbey: "I believe in Christianity as I believe that the sun has risen; not because I see it, but because by it I see everything else."

Whether or not Christian faith provides the sort of light by which we may make sense of the world, the Apostles' Creed provides a useful summary of Christian claims in a form that most Christians can accept. First, we may note that it refers to God in Trinitarian terms, as Father, Son and Holy Spirit. And that it includes an outline of the life of Jesus, emphasizing the importance of Jesus in the Christian understanding of God. Second, we may note the shape of the story that it tells: it begins with God and creation, thus claiming that all things and all people owe their existence to God. Third, it continues with the life of the Church in the present, which reminds us that Christian faith is something lived out in community with others, and that both extends back and forward through time and links us with all those who have gone before us in the faith, referred to here as the communion of saints. It also points to the importance of mutual responsibility and ethical life when it refers to the forgiveness of sins. Fourth, it points to the importance of our human embodied life both in the present and the future when it invites us to look ahead to the resurrection of the dead, and the life everlasting, the life of the world yet to come.

Each person who is invited to say the Creed may engage with it in a different way. But in a sense the claims set out in the Creed are givens, which is why we are not able to change them. We have received them from those who have gone before us, and who have helped to shape the world in which we live today. We are invited to engage with their perspective, and to see how it might help to shape or complement our own, just as we may question theirs. Not every age and every culture shares the postmodern western emphasis on the primacy and virtue of individual choice, and personal assent, that we may take for granted.

Part of what the creeds do, therefore, is to prevent us from assuming that our own personal or private understanding and practice of faith should be normative for anyone else. They remind us that the Church has public statements of faith, which do not depend on our individual assent or approval. And they invite us to explore that faith in all its fullness. To be open to what we might not yet accept or understand. And to acknowledge that our own perspective in the world is not the best or the only one.

So what do we do when we recite the Creed? Saying it together, in the context of public worship, reminds us of the core claims of the Christian faith. It invites us to reflect on what it claims. To see the world through the eyes of others as well as through our own. And to find meaning and purpose for own lives in the wider context of the story of God, and God's world, that the Creed invites us to explore.

7

When we call upon thee: Praying with and for others

The service of Evensong contains a number of different types of Christian prayer: confession, praise, thanksgiving and intercession. In different ways, they express dependence on God, or ask for God's help. Twice the service includes the Lord's Prayer, to which we will turn in Chapter 8, as the classic example of Christian prayer.

As we noted when discussing the structure of the service, Evensong begins with a penitential section in which participants are invited to confess their sins, as a prelude to what follows. This reminder of Christian beliefs about human sinfulness and frailty (or as the author Francis Spufford has memorably and helpfully characterized it, "the human propensity to [mess] things up") has a prominent place in the service, but may require some explanation. So Spufford's formulation may be a way of articulating and communicating clearly what Christian theology means by "sin", since that word itself may now hinder rather than help understanding, even if the phenomenon to which it refers is actually easily recognizable as part of human experience. If left uninterpreted, references to sin and calls to repentance can seem not only off-putting, but also unhelpfully at variance with contemporary sensibilities. Particularly in its full-throated 1662 version, the words of confession might be considered detrimental to self-esteem and wellbeing, or otherwise psychologically harmful, especially if approached as an invitation to ruminate on ways in which our lives and our world are less than perfect, and with little prospect of any positive outcome or resolution.

Yet the opposite is intended: Christians do believe in human sinfulness, or "the human propensity to [mess] things up", but also in a merciful God more ready to forgive than we are ready to repent of sin and to ask for forgiveness. Therefore a regular and repeated liturgical pattern of confession followed by a reminder or pronouncement of God's forgiveness in the form of a spoken absolution can remind us of God's mercy and offer the reassurance of a new start as often as we need it, and so contribute to our wellbeing. Both in the 1662 version of the confession and absolution, and in the alternative forms introduced in 1928, the service's call to repentance (turning our back on what is sinful, and reorientating ourselves to live in a right relationship with God and with other people) is predicated on a prior belief in God's mercy, and the liberation that such mercy and forgiveness can bring.

Shortly after this follow other prayers (spoken or sung) which ask for God's empowerment for those gathered at Evensong to worship him. Their presence at this part in the service underscores the Christian conviction that human beings are creatures who depend on God for their lives, and for all that they do—which is what many Christians mean when they speak of living in relationship to God.

Later in the service are more prayers in the form of short petitions to God. They are again used in conjunction with the Lord's Prayer, and together with it are sometimes referred to as the Lesser Litany, a litany being a sequence of intercessory prayers, often in the form of a series of petitions said by a minister followed by a congregational response.

Then follow three slightly longer prayers known as collects—a first collect or prayer for the day, and two that are always used: the Collect for Peace, and the Collect for Aid against all Perils. There is also an opportunity for the person leading the service to include other prayers at their discretion. These may include intercessions that bring before God matters of immediate and contemporary concern, written especially for the particular occasion on which they are used, that give to those present an opportunity to pray for or be reminded of the needs of others across the world as well as of themselves and others attending the service. In addition, or instead, they may include prayers taken from the Book of Common Prayer or elsewhere, including Cranmer's Prayer of General Thanksgiving. We shall consider these different prayers in turn, and some of the issues that they raise, before reflecting on the Lord's Prayer as a way of drawing together the different threads of this discussion.

In the Lesser Litany, and in the intercessions, those present are invited to look beyond themselves and their own lives to the wider world and to the needs of others as well as of themselves. The precise form of the Lesser Litany, which sometimes includes a prayer for a head of state, varies in different countries according to their constitutional arrangements. In the United States, for example, the version of the Book of Common Prayer used by the Episcopal Church omits this petition and does not replace it with anything else. In the version of the Book of Common Prayer used in the Church of Ireland, congregations in Northern Ireland pray for the monarch, as elsewhere in the United Kingdom, but those in the Republic of Ireland pray for their rulers. In the United Kingdom, those present pray for the King (or Queen), their government and all God's people, asking for "peace in our time". Here we are reminded of the Tudor political context in which the Prayer Book came into being, with its emphasis on the need for one common form of prayer as an instrument of national harmony and as a way of maintaining or imposing the sort of peace and order that the monarch desired, and that the monarch expected the national Church to foster and enforce. That is not how most of us understand the role of religious faith or worship today, or the role of the Church of England, but it makes the point that Christian worship is intended to address the realities of the world in which we live, and that worship is political because it raises questions about how people of faith engage in the public sphere with others whose needs and beliefs and customs may differ from their own.

The three collects take their name from the Latin *collecta*, meaning things gathered together. This is sometimes explained on the basis that the minister leads the people in collective worship, or that the prayers serve to gather together in an orderly way the thoughts of those who pray. Collects usually consist of a single extended sentence, with some form of petition, and finish with a statement of praise. Some of the collects found in the Book of Common Prayer are translations of older Latin collects, which is the case for the two collects always used at Evensong, the Collect for Peace and the Collect for Aid against all Perils. The former echoes a number of biblical texts (1 Corinthians 14:33; John 17:3; John 8:31-36; Romans 6:15-23; Psalm 27:1,3) and the latter echoes several psalms (Psalms 18:28; 139:11; 121:3-4 [Coverdale]). The collect for the day can be for a specific occasion, such as a saint's day or Ascension Day, or may be the collect of the week or the season in which a particular service of Evensong takes place. Some prayers used as first collects were translations from earlier Latin texts, in which case Cranmer and other reformers who translated them took care to remove direct prayer to saints, or other elements with which they disagreed. Some are Cranmer's own composition, and it is often said that he took especial care in writing or translating collects.

Although the Lesser Litany and the collects are often sung, the prayers of intercession that are included in the service are usually spoken by the officiant and are followed by an opportunity for those present to say "amen". This offers a way for all those present to give verbal expression of their assent to the prayers and to make them their own.

That these prayers are spoken can make these words feel more direct than words in prayers that are sung, and can raise similar issues to the Creed. What, we may ask, are we to make of the claims that prayers presuppose or imply, especially if they appear to make requests for God to act in the world in certain ways, or to bring about change in some way that appears to defy our understanding of how the world works? These are pressing questions, and help to explain why some people find the prayers just as difficult or more difficult than the Creed, and see them as a moment in the service during which they might disengage if they do not find the prayers a helpful basis for reflection on the topics that the prayers address. This is something of which the person leading the service needs to be mindful and to take into account if they are to be respectful of those in the congregation who do not consider themselves people who pray, as well as respectful of those who do.

One way to approach questions about what we do when we make intercessory prayers, in which we might ask God to do something, is to ask philosophical or theological questions about how God might be said to be at work in the world, and whether divine action includes the scope to change or modify natural processes in response to specific requests in the form of intercessory prayer. That would take us far beyond the scope of the book, so it is not possible here. Another way is to ask questions about what we are doing when we pray. When we pray for particular people in particular circumstances, are we really asking God to act in new ways in response to our prayers? Or are we expressing our dependence on God and bringing to God the people and things that concern us most, in a way similar to that in which we share hopes and fears with people whom we love, but whom we do not expect to act to resolve the issues that we discuss with them? Sometimes just talking with someone whom we trust may be a help, and the same can be true when we bring things to God in prayer, and find that we are seen and heard and attended to. So understood, prayer is primarily relational, not transactional.

Of course, questions remain about how God is active in the world, about whether and how prayer is answered, and about how Christian claims that God is love are to be understood in the light of all that we see in the world around us. These are questions that are not easily resolved on an intellectual level. Few Christians or other people of faith will deny the force of the evidence and arguments that explain why many people do not believe in God, even if they wish that they could, but see the physical universe as a closed system that is best explained on purely naturalistic terms that leave no need to believe in God or anything supernatural. There can be no doubt that increased scientific understanding of the world makes God an unnecessary hypothesis, but that is not the same as proving that God does not exist. Thus even when familiar with the arguments that prevent others from believing in or praying to God, Christians and others may find that their religious faith remains intact. At least in part, this may be because they do not believe that God is a thing that can be measured or weighed, like a specimen in a laboratory, but only encountered when they step out in faith, even if questions remain, and find that God is there and able to hold them when they pray and place their trust in him.

For those who have this experience, it coheres with a Christian understanding of the world and their place in it. But it may have little persuasive power for those who do not share the experience, or a religious explanation of it, so it may never be good enough reason for someone without that experience to come to religious faith. What makes sense to the person within the community of faith may be difficult to convey in meaningful terms to those looking in from a different perspective. This challenge serves as a reminder of differences between those who appreciate Evensong as Christian worship and those who appreciate it on aesthetic but exclusively naturalistic terms.

Such differences are important to acknowledge, if we are to respect the integrity of those who express religious faith and the integrity of those who do not. However, rather than dwell on abstract questions, whether from the perspective of someone who prays or someone who does not, it may be helpful to focus on the Lord's Prayer in order to ask what Christians do when they pray. This text is central to the Christian understanding of prayer, features twice in Evensong, and is the subject of the following chapter.

8

The prayer that Jesus gave us: The Lord's Prayer and Christian spirituality

The Lord's Prayer originates in teaching that Jesus gave and is found in two different forms in the New Testament. In the shorter form, found in the Gospel according to Luke, Jesus gives the prayer to his disciples when they ask him to teach them how to pray (Luke 11:1–4). In its longer and more widely used form, which is the basis for the form in which it appears in Choral Evensong, Jesus introduces the prayer in his Sermon on the Mount, when he teaches his disciples how to pray (Matthew 6:9–13).

It's unclear whether Jesus expected his disciples to recite these words formally as a set prayer in the way that we often do, including twice at Evensong, or if he offered them more as a general framework in which his followers might structure their prayers. I don't suppose that it matters, and the prayer may be used as is, or as a template for more extended prayer. Either way, it offers a succinct summary of Jesus' teaching about how those who follow him should relate both to God and to other people.

Many people find it difficult to pray, so having words that they know by heart can be useful. This is part of the reason why Christians have often been encouraged to memorize this prayer. If prayer feels like a struggle, or we don't know how to express ourselves, the Lord's Prayer gives us a model or a pattern that we may use. It also takes us to the heart of core Christian beliefs about who God is and how Jesus invites people to relate to God as his heavenly father and as ours.

Right from the start, the Lord's Prayer makes bold claims about God, and how we might relate to him: *Our Father, which art in heaven, hallowed be thy name.* There, in that very first short word "our", we are reminded that we address God not simply as individuals, but as people who are bound up in relationships with other people as well as with God.

And we address God in an explicitly relational way. A way that is intimate and direct, yet acknowledges God's priority over us. God is our Father, and we are God's children. For some of us, of course, father may be a problematic word. Fathers can abuse and neglect their children, and some of us may have suffered from that, or may know other people who have. Perhaps we may find it easier to think of God as like a mother rather than like a father, and there are texts in the Bible that do just that. That compare God to a mother eagle looking after her chicks (Deuteronomy 32:11). To a mother bear attacking a lion to protect her cubs (Hosea 13:8). To a woman in labour (Isaiah 42:14). To a mother feeding her child at her breast (Psalm 131:2; cf. Isaiah 49:15: 66:13).

None of this, of course, means to say that God is a woman any more than God is a man. God is neither, and key to it all is an analogy: that God is like a parent, but a parent better than any human parent we know. For many of us with good and loving parents, God is like them both, only better. For those of us who don't see our parents as people to look up to, for those of us whose relationships with our parents is bad, then God is better than even the best sort of parent we imagine or long for.

Yet God our Father *is in heaven.* Though we may address him in this tender and intimate way as our Father, God remains entirely other and beyond our grasp, beyond our comprehension. We are not to invoke his name lightly, but to honour it, as we should honour God.

God is in heaven, and we are on earth. But the God who is in heaven sent Jesus not only to proclaim but also to embody his kingdom, his kingly rule over all creation. And Jesus tells to pray for that day when that kingly rule will be fully seen: *Thy kingdom come, thy will be done on earth as it is in heaven.*

Jesus's words encourage us to keep a vision of heaven before us, so that we may have confidence as we pray and as we work for peace and justice here on earth. So that we may work towards a world where sorrow and death are no more. A world where all have an equal share in the good things of God's creation, and where God is given his rightful place at the centre of all that we do. The Lord's Prayer invites us to lift our hearts and minds to heaven, but in order to encourage us to seek to transform the world, not to escape from it.

Thus the Lord's Prayer invites us to express our dependence on God for the basic things that we need, both in material and relational terms. *Give us this day our daily bread.* We ask for God's help, and so we express our dependence on God. For some of us, this may be hard. We may not like to acknowledge that we rely on anyone else, and some of the time we can fool ourselves that we don't. But Jesus invites us to express our dependence on God, the ultimate provider of all that we need to flourish, and on other people too.

Thus we ask God to *Forgive us our trespasses as we forgive those who trespass against us.* We ask that God will forgive our shortcomings and acknowledge that we should show the same generosity and forgiveness to others. God's will is not yet done on earth as it is in heaven, so all of us must deal with the reality of the world as it is, of human relationships as they are, even as we pray and work for God's kingdom to come.

But to acknowledge that everything comes from God raises questions about why bad things happen, and where God might be in them. All of us face testing and trial in different ways, and Jesus seems to say that ultimately it too is under God's control: *Lead us not into temptation*, or better perhaps, *Lead us not into the time of trial*, which more accurately reflects his meaning. *But deliver us from evil.*

Jesus puts the ultimate responsibility for everything that happens upon God, and encourages us to pray not only that we may escape the time of trial, but that God will deliver us from evil. Faith does nor shelter us from the suffering that we see in the world, and God will not always give us what we might pray for. But these words that Jesus invites us to pray remind us that no matter what happens, God remains in control. Jesus himself was brought to a time of trial, when he was tempted in the wilderness, and again in the Garden of Gethsemane, but by God's grace he came through those times of testing.

Christian prayer brings us out of ourselves. It focuses us on God, encourages us to express our dependence on him, reminds us of our interdependence on other people, and emboldens us to work for the very things for which we pray. Sometimes, or even often, it may feel like a struggle. But sometimes even in darkness we may see a glimmer of light and know God's blessing, as we use these words to help us to place ourselves in relation to God and to the world around us. *For God's is the kingdom, the power and the glory, for ever and ever. Amen.*

The prayer that Jesus gave us

Further discussions of the Lord's Prayer include Tom Wright, *The Lord and his Prayer* (London: SPCK, 2012) and the study guide, by Paula Gooder and others, *Pilgrim: The Lord's Prayer* (London: Church House Publishing, 2013).

The Lord's Prayer is also discussed in commentaries on the Gospel according to Matthew, and in the Gospel according to Luke, since it is included in each of these two gospels, but with some variations in their wording. William M. Wright considers both versions alongside each other in *The Lord's Prayer (Touchstone Texts): Matthew 6 and Luke 11 for the Life of the Church* (Grand Rapids, MI: Baker Academic, 2023).

For an academic survey of how the Lord's Prayer has been used and interpreted from the early Church to the modern day, see Kenneth W. Stevenson, *The Lord's Prayer: A Text in Tradition* (London: SCM Press, 2004).

Conclusion

Work of art and act of worship

One of the features of religious faith, or religious practice, is that it makes most sense when experienced or understood or practiced from within, from the perspective of a participant—not as seen by a neutral observer, but as lived by someone who is shaped by the claims that it makes, and the practices and commitments that it entails.

This can be seen in worship, which is perhaps the most prominent way in which people of different faiths create or cultivate the sort of space in which religious claims make sense. It is in acts of worship that religious communities create a communal practice in which people reflect on the claims of their faith, often with reference to sacred texts, and on what those claims say about the wider world, and the place of an individual or community in it. Choral Evensong offers one example of this wider phenomenon, in a distinctively Christian and Anglican form, as we have noted in this book.

For those who engage in Evensong as an act of Christian worship, it offers a structured time-bound space when participants sing or hear or speak words that set out Christian claims about God, and about the difference that commitment to God, or belief in God, can make to the way in which they live their lives. Its non-demanding approach allows a gentle way in, but its capacious structure and the breadth of texts that it includes also allows those who participate to engage robustly with the claims of Christian faith and to find sustenance for spiritual growth.

Seen from outside, from the perspective of someone who does not believe in those claims, and does not seek to live in the light of them, those claims may be construed as false, as damaging, or as worse. Praising God for God's mighty acts, or for God's goodness or love, may seem no better than wishful thinking, or an attempt at evading or ignoring evidence for human suffering and other problems that we see and experience in the world around us.

Seen from inside, however, reminding ourselves of God's goodness and justice and love, and praying for ourselves and for others in need, can be a life-changing experience, in which we are inspired to work for the transformation of the world around us, just as we find that the God to whom we pray is at work transforming us.

As the writer Karen Armstrong has put it, "Religion is a form of practical knowledge, like driving ... You cannot learn to drive by reading the car manual or the Highway Code; you have to get into vehicle and learn to manipulate the brakes. The rules of a board game sound obscure and dull until you start to play, and then everything falls into place. There are some things that can be learned only by constant, dedicated practice."

"Religion too", she continues, "is a practical discipline in which we learn new capacities of mind and heart." If we are truly to understand it, we need to try it, and to see what happens when we do.

Not everyone who attends or enjoys Evensong will accept the religious claims that underpin it, and it is a service perhaps uniquely accessible to agnostics, atheists and nones, as well as to those who identify as having religious faith. I hope that this book has been a helpful guide to the service, both for those who come to it as an act of worship, and for those who appreciate it as a spiritual resource, whatever they may make think of the religious claims that it makes.

For further thought

Introduction

Richard Dawkins made this comment in an interview published in the *Spectator* on 14 September 2003. There he observes: "I suppose I'm a cultural Anglican, and I see evensong in a country church through much the same eyes as I see a village cricket match on the village green. I have a certain love for it." <https://www.spectator.co.uk/article/richard-dawkins-interview-i-have-a-certain-love-for-the-anglican-tradition-/>, accessed 27 March 2025.

Richard Coles's novel, *Murder Before Evensong* (London: Weidenfeld and Nicolson, 2022) is billed as the first in his Canon Clement Mystery Series. The title may be compared to Douglas Clark's murder mystery, published independently in 2018, as *Death after Evensong*.

The music critic is Tom Service, and his article about a visit to Lincoln Cathedral was published in the *Guardian* on 8 December 2009. <https://www.theguardian.com/music/tomserviceblog/2009/dec/08/choral-evensong-lincoln-cathedral>, accessed 27 March 2025.

Diarmaid MacCulloch discusses the service in his introduction to the Everyman's Library edition of the Book of Common Prayer (London: Random House, 2009). The quotation is from p. xxiii.

Work of art and act of worship

The website for BBC Radio Three Choral Evensong may be found at <https://www.bbc.co.uk/programmes/b006tp7r>, accessed 27 March 2025.

The website www.choralevensong.org offers links to services of Evensong streamed from around Britain and Ireland, and also a brief introduction to the service and the musical repertoire on which it draws.

Performance or participation

The quotation from Jonathan Arnold about his experience at York Minister comes from his book *Sacred Music in Secular Society* (Farnham: Ashgate, 2014), p. xiv.

Here, in conversation with professional composers and performers of sacred music (not all of whom identify as religious), as well as with a Christian theologian and with a Christian philosopher, Arnold draws on his own experience and theirs to reflect on the status and appeal of sacred music in both liturgical and secular settings. He considers why sacred music is popular in contemporary western society, appealing to both religious and non-religious listeners, even when much organised religion (and much church attendance) is on the wane. Such music, he argues, when sung well, brings spiritual benefit to its performers and listeners both in the context of Christian worship and in a secular concert performance – which, he suggests, raises questions about what is meant by 'the sacred'.

In a companion volume, *Music and Faith: Conversations in a Post-Secular Age* (Woodbridge: Boydell, 2019) Arnold engages with a wider circle of people, not just professional musicians and academics. He interviews a range of people who listen to sacred music, whether in church, in a concert, or through recordings, and who have an interest in how that music might connect with faith (whether that interest includes personal faith or belief or not). Music and faith, he concludes:

> are so closely aligned that the experience of one can evoke the other, or the two can be virtually indistinguishable. Music deepens, nourishes and enhances faith. It can also challenge and disturb our faith. Faith enriches music, accompanies and embraces it. ... Religious practice, ritual and performance and engagement are all part of the story, and music is part of a bigger picture of divine gift and encounter through nature, a

> gift that God continues to give and one that is
> available everywhere. (p.230)

Michael Sadgrove's reflections on Choral Evensong are found on his blog "Woolgathering in North East England": <http://northernwoolgatherer.blogspot.com>. His reflections on Choral Evensong are dated 2 October 2016.

The quotation from the Coventry Cathedral website is from an old version, now replaced by the new website that was built in 2022.

Structure and language

The historian of church music is Erik Routley. The quotation about the script of Choral Evensong comes from his book, republished with additional material by Lionel Daker, *A Short History of English Church Music* (London: Mowbray, 1997), p.58.

Charles Hefling applies the idea of a script or playbook to the whole Book of Common Prayer, which allows us to see Choral Evensong as one of the acts that the Prayer Book contains. Its script allows its actors to know in advance what will happen next, and how they can perform or pray together in an orderly fashion. See Charles Hefling, "Introduction: Anglicans and Common Prayer", in Charles Hefling and Cynthia Shattuck (eds), *The Oxford Guide to the Book of Common Prayer: A*

Worldwide Survey (Oxford: Oxford University Press, 2006), pp. 1–6, on p. 1.

The earlier commentators on the Prayer Book from whom I quote in this chapter are Charles Neil and K. M. Willoughby, editors of *The Tutorial Prayer Book* (London: Church Room Book Press, 1959), p. 108.

More recent guides to the Book of Common Prayer include Charles Hefling, *The Book of Common Prayer: A Guide* (Oxford: Oxford University Press, 2021); Brian Cummings, *The Book of Common Prayer: A Very Short Introduction* (Oxford: Oxford University Press, 2018), and Charles Hefling and Cynthia Shattuck (eds), *The Oxford Guide to the Book of Common Prayer: A Worldwide Survey* (Oxford: Oxford University Press, 2006). Different editions of the Book of Common Prayer are set out and discussed in Brian Cummings (ed.), *The Book of Common Prayer: The Texts of 1549, 1559 and 1662* (Oxford: Oxford University Press, 2013).

For the continual reading of Scripture

Useful introductions to the Bible include John Riches, *The Bible: A Very Short Introduction* (Oxford: Oxford University Press, 2021) and John Barton, *A History of the Bible: The Book and its Faiths* (London: Penguin Books, 2020). On the New Testament, see Luke Timothy Johnson, *The New Testament: A Very Short Introduction* (Oxford: Oxford University Press, 2010).

On the use of the Magnificat and Nunc Dimittis to guide the response of those present at Evensong to the first and second lessons, Francis Proctor and Walter H. Frere write as follows, in their *A New History of the Book of Common Prayer* (London: MacMillan Press, 1925), p. 402:

> The Canticles ... occupy a most important part in the service. After reading the Old Testament, we have the song of Mary, testifying to the fulfilment of God's promise of mercy to the Fathers; and after reading ... from the New Testament, and there beholding how the promises were fulfilled in the propagation of the Gospel among the Gentiles we express our readiness to receive that Gospel for ourselves, in the Song of the aged Simeon, and our faith that by so doing we shall have peace in our death, for which every night brings a type in sleep.

Said or sung

For a brief discussion of the history of psalm singing in England, see Andrew Gant, *O Sing unto the Lord: A History of English Church Music* (London: Profile Books, 2015), where on p. 79 he discusses the use of psalms in the medieval and Reformation England on p. 79, and on p. 357 notes the importance of Nicholson.

As Gant observes, the widespread use of Nicholson's *Parish Psalter*, and the demise of the older *Cathedral Psalter* which it superseded, meant the demise "of any real sense that psalm-chanting belonged to the congregation". "Today", he notes, "it is a polished art, for many musicians the ultimate test of a church choir's skill and sensitivity to text and the bedrock of all that it does" (p. 357).

Nicholson's own explanation of his approach may still be heard in his own voice, on one of his gramophone recordings, issued by the Royal School of Church Music in 1931. There, he explains, his key principle is as follows: "freedom in the music, so that the words may be recited as they are in plain speech, without distortion of false emphasis . . . the same syllables receive the same emphasis when sung as when spoken." This recording is now available on YouTube, as part of the Archive of Recorded Church Music, curated by Colin Raphael Brownlee, at <https://www.youtube.com/@ ArchiveofRecordedChurchMusic>, accessed 28 March 2025.

Discussions of the importance of Coverdale's translation of the Psalms, including his distinctive use of prose rhythm include Sue Gillingham, *The Psalms through the Centuries: A Reception History*, Volume 1, Wiley Blackwell Bible Commentaries (Chichester: Wiley Blackwell, 2012), pp. 135–6.

On the influence of Cranmer's use of prose rhythm throughout the Book of Common Prayer (including in his collects, used towards the end of Evensong—see below Chapter 8), see Ian Robinson, *The Establishment of Modern English Prose in the Reformation and Enlightenment* (Cambridge: Cambridge University Press, 1998), pp. 82–6.

I have found the work of Walter Brueggemann very helpful in thinking about how to approach calls for vengeance in the psalms, and for his awareness of the need for Christians to think about how and why they use Jewish texts in Christian worship. He packs a great deal into his very short book, *Praying the Psalms: Engaging Scripture and the Life of Faith*, 2nd edn (Eugene, OR: Cascade Books, 2007). There he writes, on p. 52, "Few of us have lamented in Babylon or been close enough to the ovens when they have been heated."

Other accessible introductions to the psalms include a commentary by Brueggemann, co-written with William Bellinger, *Psalms*, New Cambridge Bible Commentary (Cambridge: Cambridge University Press, 2014). See also Megan Daffern, *Songs of the Spirit: A Psalm a Day for Lent and Easter* (London: SPCK, 2017), in which she introduces and discusses a carefully selected range of psalms. At much greater length, Sue Gillingham provides an overview of the long history of the use of psalms by Jews and Christians in *Psalms through the Centuries: A Reception History*, Wiley Blackwell Bible Commentaries, 3 volumes (Chichester: Wiley Blackwell, 2012, 2018 and 2022).

The phrase "texts of terror" is an allusion to the book of that name, by Phyllis Trible: *Texts of Terror: Literary Feminist Readings of Biblical Narratives* (Minneapolis, MN: Fortress Press: 2022), first published in 1982 and now republished in a 40th-anniversary edition. In it Trible discusses horrifying stories in the Bible that portray violence against women without any overt or apparent condemnation either by God or the narrator.

The quotation from John Donne (1572–1631) is from the seventeenth Meditation in his *Devotions upon Emergent Occasions*, a series of prose texts that he wrote in 1623, while recovering from a fever. This famous quotation is from the same paragraph from which another famous quotation is also often extracted:

No man is an island, entire of itself; every man is a piece of the continent, a part of the main; if a clod be washed away by the sea, Europe is the less, as well as if a promontory were, as well as if a manor of thy friend's or of thine own were; any man's death diminishes me, because I am involved in mankind, and therefore never send to know for whom the bell tolls; it tolls for thee.

Rehearse the articles of thy belief

For an introduction to the Apostles' Creed, including its historical origins, and how we might approach it today, see Alister McGrath, *The Landscape of Faith: An Explorer's Guide to the Christian Creeds* (London: SPCK, 2018). He also discusses the Nicene Creed (which is not used in Evensong) and presents both creeds as maps to the landscape of faith.

On faith as trust, and having confidence in the God in whom we place our trust, see Rowan Williams, *Tokens of Trust* (Norwich: Canterbury Press, 2007), especially pp. 4–7. This short and luminous book is an excellent introduction to the Apostles' Creed and to the nature of Christian belief. It is based on a series of talks on the essential of what Christians believe that were given at Canterbury Cathedral, and it retains the conversational style of those talks.

As Williams explains in his introduction, on p. viii, "Basic to everything here is the idea that Christian belief is really about knowing who and what to trust. I shall be suggesting that Christianity asks you to trust the God it talks about before it asks you to sign up to a complete system."

For discussion of the relationship between faith, belief and trust, and the relationship of faith to other topics (including God, reason and morality), see Roger Trigg, *Faith: A Very Short Introduction* (Oxford: Oxford University Press, 2024).

For an incisive and illuminating account of the nature of belief (both religious and non-religious), and of how beliefs 'actively shape the way in which we see and experience the world, and the way in which we enact our lives', see Alister McGrath, *Why We Believe: Finding Meaning in Uncertain Times* (London: Oneworld Publications, 2025), quotation on p. 108.

On the creeds as public statements of faith, which do not depend on the assent or approval of any one individual, see McGrath, *The Landscape of Faith*, pp. 29–30, and Williams, *Tokens of Trust*, pp. 6–7.

The inscription on C. S. Lewis's memorial is taken from "Is Theology Poetry?", one of several essays in a collection now entitled *The Weight of Glory* (London: William Collins, 2013). It is based on a paper that he gave as a lecture at the meeting of an Oxford society called The Socratic Club. The following extract gives a sense of the wider context in which these words are found:

> I was taught at school, when I had done a sum, to "prove my answer". The proof or verification of my Christian answer to the cosmic sum is this. When I accept Theology I may find difficulties, at this point or that, in harmonizing it with some particular truths which are imbedded in the mythical cosmology derived from science. But I can get in, or allow for, science as a whole. Granted that Reason is prior to matter and that

the light of the primal Reason illuminates finite minds, I can understand how men should come by observation and inference, to know a lot about the universe they live in. If, on the other hand, I swallow the scientific cosmology as a whole, then not only can I not fit in Christianity, but I cannot even fit in science. If minds are wholly dependent on brains, and brains on bio-chemistry, and bio-chemistry (in the long run) on the meaningless flux of the atoms, I cannot understand how the thought of those minds should have any more significance than the sound of the wind in the trees. And this is to me the final test. This is how I distinguish dreaming and waking. When I am awake I can, in some degree, account for and study my dream. The dragon that pursued me last night can be fitted into my waking world. I know that there are such things as dreams: I know that I had eaten an indigestible dinner: I know that a man of my reading might be expected to dream of dragons. But while in the nightmare I could not have fitted in my waking experience. The waking world is judged more real because it can thus contain the dreaming world: the dreaming world is judged less real because it cannot contain the waking one. For the same reason I am certain that in passing from the scientific point of view to the theological, I have passed from dream to waking. Christian theology can fit in science, art, morality, and the sub-Christian religions. The scientific point of view cannot fit in any of these things, not even science itself. I believe in Christianity as I believe that the Sun has risen not only because I see it but because by it I see everything else.

When we call upon thee

Francis Spufford offers this formulation in his book, *Unapologetic: Why, Despite Everything, Christianity Can Still Make Surprising Emotional Sense* (London: Faber & Faber, 2012), but in stronger language than I used in my quotation. Where I inserted [mess] he wrote "f**k". This phrase, "the human propensity to f**k things up" he abbreviates with the acronym 'HPtFTU' and he discusses the concept to which it refers on pp. 27–8. He uses this expression to avoid religious language that many people find off-putting, but is at pains to explain, in non-religious terms, how it refers to an experience or a phenomenon to which most of us can readily relate. As Spufford explains:

> what we're talking about here is not just our tendency to lurch and stumble and screw up by accident, our passive role as agents of entropy. It's our active inclination to break stuff, 'stuff' here

> including moods, promises, relationships we
> care about, and our own well-being and other
> people's, as well as material objects whose high
> gloss positively seems to invite a big fat scratch.

The claim that God is not another thing, or not even another being, and therefore not comparable with other things or beings, is an important part of Christian theology, and shared with other faiths. It has recently found fresh expression in the work of Rupert Shortt, whose short book makes this point in its title: *God is No Thing: Coherent Christianity* (London: C. Hurst & Co., 2016).

In this book, he argues, "if God is no thing", God is neither "an agent whose actions compete with those of other agents" (p. 15) nor "an expedient for plugging our shrinking gaps in our knowledge" (p. 16). Thus Shortt responds to the criticism that Christians worship a God who is no more than a projection of the wish for a heavenly moral policeman or a heavenly Father Christmas, depending on the preferences of the person imagining God in either way. His book is written, he notes "especially for those who find the creeds unpalatable or plain boring" (p. 14) and offers an account of Christian faith that is both intellectually sophisticated and practical in its shape and outlook. As Shortt observes, "The book defends a way of life, not a scientific theory such as evolution, nor an abstract term like liberty. Whatever view you take of my theme, it cannot be divorced from the personal commitment that gives it meaning . . . You don't think your way into a new way of living, but live your way into a new way of thinking. Being a Christian should not entail assenting to six impossible propositions before breakfast, but doing things that change you" (p. 13).

Praying with and for others

Useful suggestions about ways in which to pray, suitable both for beginners and for those interested in exploring new approaches, may be found in John Pritchard, *How to Pray: A Practical Handbook* (London: SPCK, 2011) and *How Do I Pray? A Little Book of Guidance* (London: SPCK, 2015).

For a rigorous philosophical analysis of questions about the nature and practice of prayer, see Vincent Brümmer, *What Are We Doing When We Pray? On Prayer and the Nature of Faith* (Abingdon: Routledge, 2016; first published in this revised edition by in 2008 by Ashgate Publishing). Some similar ground is covered, in a more popular form, in David Wilkinson, *When I pray, what does God do?* (Oxford: Monarch, 2015). "This book," he writes, "is not an attempt to provide a definitive answer to how God answers prayer. It is more a record of a personal and ongoing journey of how a Christian who wants to take both the Bible and science seriously begins to think about these things" (p.

36). Among the topics that it addresses is how the Bible portrays God answering prayer, how we might pray in the light of what we think that God is doing already, and how we might respond to our experience of unanswered prayer.

On questions about how God is at work in the world, see David Wilkinson, *How Does God Act in the World? Science, Miracle and Mission* (Eugene, OR: Cascade Books, 2025), and John Polkinghorne, *Science and Providence: God's Interaction with the World* (London: SPCK, 1989), which includes a chapter on prayer.

Conclusion

The quotations from Karen Armstrong come from a short essay that she published in the *New Statesman*, in a special issue on religion, dated 22–28 March 2013. A fuller version of her argument is set out in her book, *The Case for God: What Religion Really Means* (London: Bodley Head, 2009), most notably in her introduction and conclusion to that work.

EU GPSR Authorized Representative:

LOGOS EUROPE, 9 rue Nicolas Poussin, 17000 La Rochelle, France

contact@logoseurope.eu

www.ingramcontent.com/pod-product-compliance
Lightning Source LLC
Chambersburg PA
CBHW060423090426
42734CB00011B/2429